Love Is a Red Balloon

Love Is
A Red Balloon

By Dean Walley

Photographs by
Harv Gariety

♛ Hallmark Editions

Love Is
A Red Balloon

Love Is a Red Balloon

Loving wisely and loving well
sound like strange bedfellows to me.
Wisdom is balanced checkbooks,
regular hours,
self-discipline,
prudent talk,
sensible shoes.

And love is a red balloon.

Near Miss

The thing of it is,
when you think you do,
she is thinking she doesn't...

...and when you begin to think she doesn't
and never will,
she is starting to think she does,
at which point you start thinking
you don't anymore.

Resolution

Never again, I tell myself.
It's better to be alone on the shelf.
Never the wonder.
It's not worth the pain.
While I look for rainbows,
I drown in the rain.
Never the trouble and never the sorrow.
Never again...
well...
maybe tomorrow.

7 A.M.

The first time you saw
my early-morning face,
rumpled, wrinkled, whiskered,
I thought the whole thing was over...

...but then you kissed me,
soft as sun through fog,
and I knew that the whole thing
had just begun.

Crazy Love

I want to be wild and free
and make crazy love to you.
I want to stay up all night
getting drunk on the wine of us....

We can share one tube of toothpaste
and squeeze it in the middle...

...and strew our bed
with cracker crumbs
and love.

Brrrrrrr!

Cold feet
are two more reasons
for missing you.

God Bless
Alexander Graham Bell!

God bless Alexander Graham Bell!
I hope that he's in heaven smiling now
with the knowledge
that his brainchild
spanned a continent tonight,
bringing the words I needed...

..."Please hurry home!"

"I'll meet you at the airport!"

"I love you
very much!"

Picnic

It doesn't take much to make me happy.
If you forget to bring the jug of wine,
the loaf of bread,
I'll fill up on thou.

2 A.M.

When you wake in the night,
cold,

sometimes afraid...

...I love to pull you warm and safe
against me
and go back to sleep,
feeling stronger than Superman,
as happy as God.

Cold Cut

You say you think you love me,
and that sounds nice—but phony:
Love either is—or not at all—
and thinking is baloney!

Do Not Pass Go

I could play Monopoly with you
all night long
and not even care if you always
got Boardwalk and Park Place...

...but I don't want to play
   Hard to Get...
   Wait and See...
   Where Were You?...
   Promise Me—
the loveless games
that neither one of us
can ever win.

Midnight Sun

I love you
warm as morning sun
and sometimes hot as noon in August...

...and that passion doesn't die,

for, like the sun,

it only sets on part of me...

...and in the darkness,

afterwards,

it's shining still

in other countries of my heart.

Starshine

I didn't turn around in time
to see the falling star,
but I saw the wish in your eyes
and knew
   that it was about to come true.

Home Movie

My mind made a movie
of the two of us last night
when everything was beautiful
and all the wrongs were right....

If tomorrow takes the beautiful
and you away from me,
at least I'll have an old-time movie
on my spools of memory.

Monologue

If you would only listen.
My words just seem to bounce off you
like beach balls.
I'd shake you
if I thought that would get your attention.

   What's that?
      I didn't hear you.

We Fit!

The world is a great big puzzle
broken apart like Humpty Dumpty,
with so many pieces missing,
unworkable...

...but now

two of those pieces are interlocked

in love.

We've done what all the King's horses

and all the King's men could never do.

We've put our world together again.

All the Every Loves

I've loved Mother and Dad,
two ducks named Gary and Larry,
and a silver compass on a silver chain....

I've loved comic books,
and climbing trees,
and that sudden feeling
when summer flips over into fall.
I've loved God
and the U. S. of A.,
and Mother's cherry pie
(she never had much luck
with apple)....

And I've loved the idea of love
and the feel of loving.
But I knew there had to be more—
more to love—
more love in me to give....

Then I found you.
And all the old loves were new again
within the perfect circle of our love,
soaring
as high as a red balloon.

Set in Jeannette, a light informal script,
designed exclusively for Hallmark
by Hermann Zapf. Typography by
Hallmark Photo Composition.
Printed on Hallmark Crown Royale paper.
Book design by William M. Gilmore.